TO THE FRONT!

Clara Barton Braves the Battle of Antietam

Claudia Friddell

Illustrated by

Christopher Cyr

CALKINS CREEK

AN IMPRINT OF ASTRA BOOKS FOR YOUNG READERS

New York

This is my homage to Clara Barton and her
timeless words that call for compassion and humanity.
In tribute, I have blended Clara's words (set in *blue or brown bold italics*)
with mine (set in plain font).
—CF

*B*ut here was to begin a new experience for me. I was to ride 80 miles in an army-wagon, and straight into battle and danger at that. I could take no female companion—no friend, but the stout working men I had use for.

Clara's wagon
filled with supplies
heads for Antietam.

Clara's wagon
ten miles back
trails a slow-moving mass.

Clara's wagon
waiting for darkness
sneaks on past them.

Clara's wagon
ten miles by sunrise
leading the pass.

You must know that we had passed the supplies the night before;
they could not come up until the fate of the day was decided.
Those are their orders;
They must not risk falling into the hands of the enemy.
[I could] succor the wounded
until the medical aid and supplies should come up.

I could run the risk;
it made no difference to any one if I were shot or taken prisoner.

On the evening of the 16th of September
we reached the valley of Antietam.
It was a miserable night. . . .

We knew,
every one knew,
that two great armies of 80,000 men
were lying there face to face,
only waiting for dawn to begin the battle.

Before dawn I went up on the hill,
and there I could sweep the country with my glass,
see the countless watchfires of both armies,
lying face to face,
ready to spring,
yet not a man to be seen.

Before I left the hill,
the dawn came,
and the firing began away on the right.

There was to be the beginning of the battle,
and there I should be needed first.

Clara's men,
always her helpers,
follow the cannon
searching for wounded.

Clara's men,
always her helpers,
winding through cornfields
finding the wounded.

Clara's men,
always her helpers,
manning the barnyard
tending to wounded.

Clara's men,
always her helpers,
filling the farmhouse,
so many wounded.

Clara's men,
. . . always her helpers.

The wounded kept pouring in,
and we kept working over them.

A man lying upon the ground asked for drink.
I stooped to give it
and having raised him with my right hand
was holding the cup to his lips with my left—
when I felt a sudden twitch of the loose sleeve of my dress. . . .

A ball had passed between my body,
and the right arm which supported him—
cutting through the sleeve—and passing thru his chest
from shoulder to shoulder.
There was no more to be done for him
and I left him to his rest.

I have never mended that hole in my sleeve. I wonder
if a soldier ever does mend a bullet hole in his coat.

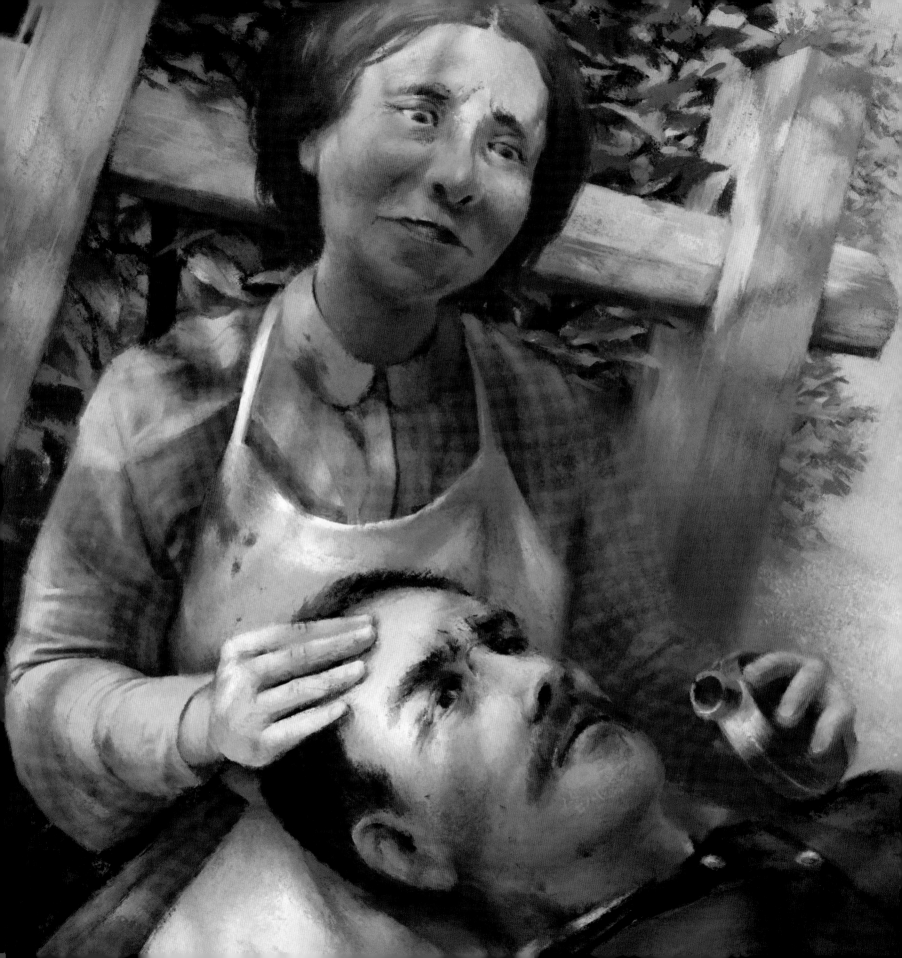

Clara's hands,
like wings,
swoop down
to lift the fallen.

Clara's hands,
like cups,
reach out
to feed the hungry.

Clara's hands,
like tools,
dig deep
to mend the broken.

Clara's hands,
like prayers,
hold hope
to soothe the suffering.

I followed [my men] through the corn,
and came upon the house.

It had a high, broad verandah,
and on this
every kind of a thing
that pretended to be a table was standing,

and on the tables were the poor men,
and beside them the surgeons.

The doctor warns Clara,
There's no hope for us!

The doctor begs Clara,
Please have mercy on us!

The doctor asks Clara,
Have you supplies for us?

The doctor thanks Clara,
Angel, you have blessed us!

It's a curious thing that happens
when Clara sees miles and miles
of hungry masses.

It's a curious thing that happens
when they cut the last loaf of bread
and pound the last cracker.

It's a curious thing that happens
when Clara feels Indian meal, not sawdust,
packed around bottles.

It's a curious thing that happens
when Clara finds salt and more meal
stashed in the cellar.

It's a curious thing that happens
when Clara stirs miracles into meals—
hundreds and hundreds of meals.

Oh yes!
cries Clara to her men.
It's a curious thing that happened,
and a lucky thing too.

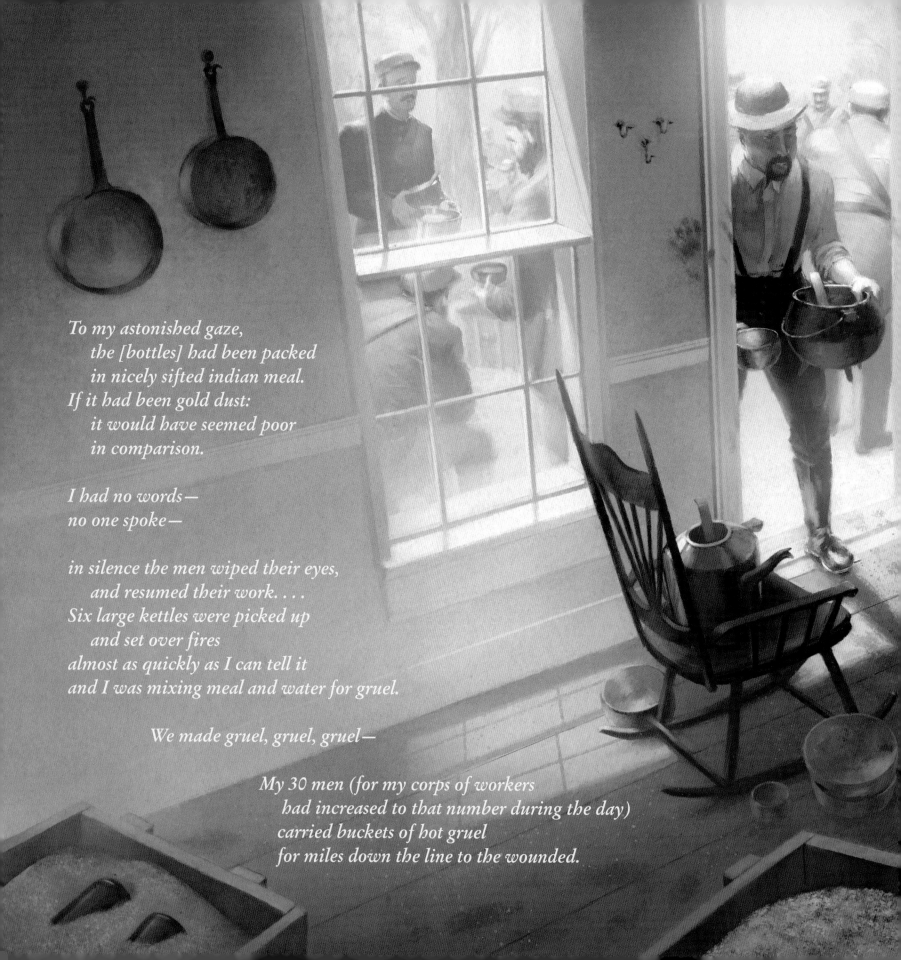

To my astonished gaze,
   the [bottles] had been packed
   in nicely sifted indian meal.
If it had been gold dust:
   it would have seemed poor
   in comparison.

I had no words—
no one spoke—

in silence the men wiped their eyes,
   and resumed their work. . . .
Six large kettles were picked up
   and set over fires
almost as quickly as I can tell it
and I was mixing meal and water for gruel.

   We made gruel, gruel, gruel—

   My 30 men (for my corps of workers
      had increased to that number during the day)
      carried buckets of hot gruel
         for miles down the line to the wounded.

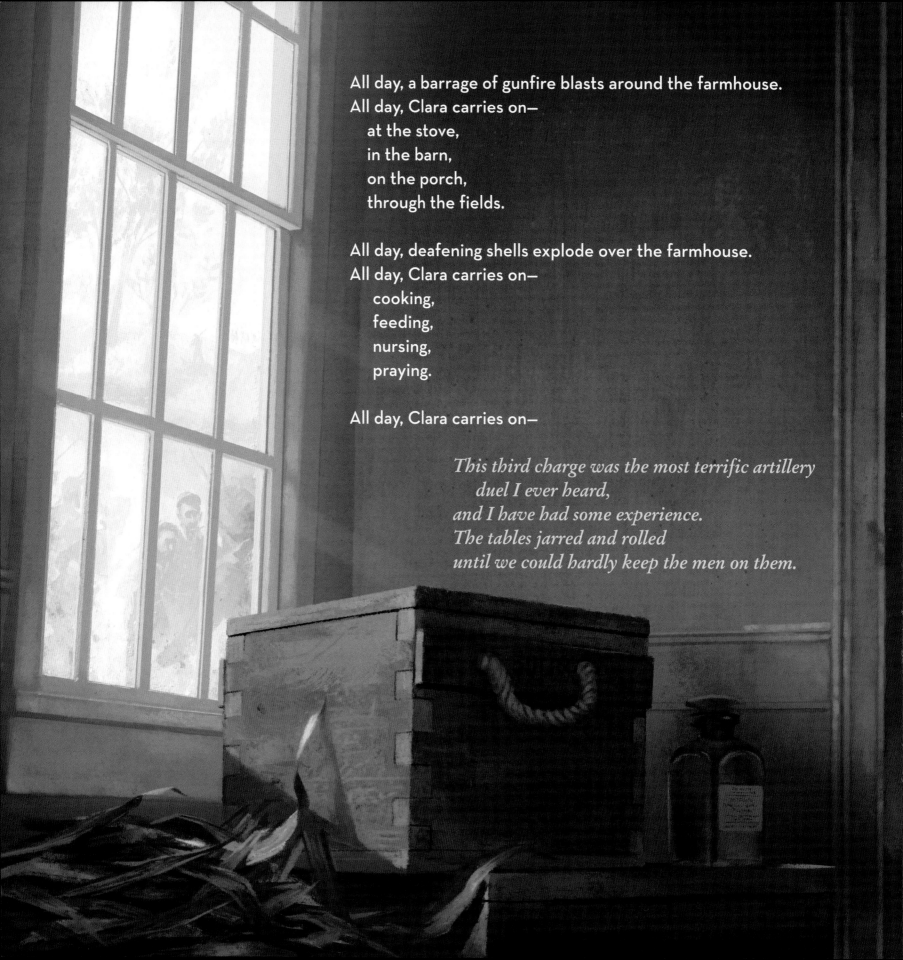

All day, a barrage of gunfire blasts around the farmhouse.
All day, Clara carries on—
    at the stove,
    in the barn,
    on the porch,
    through the fields.

All day, deafening shells explode over the farmhouse.
All day, Clara carries on—
    cooking,
    feeding,
    nursing,
    praying.

All day, Clara carries on—

This third charge was the most terrific artillery
    duel I ever heard,
and I have had some experience.
The tables jarred and rolled
until we could hardly keep the men on them.

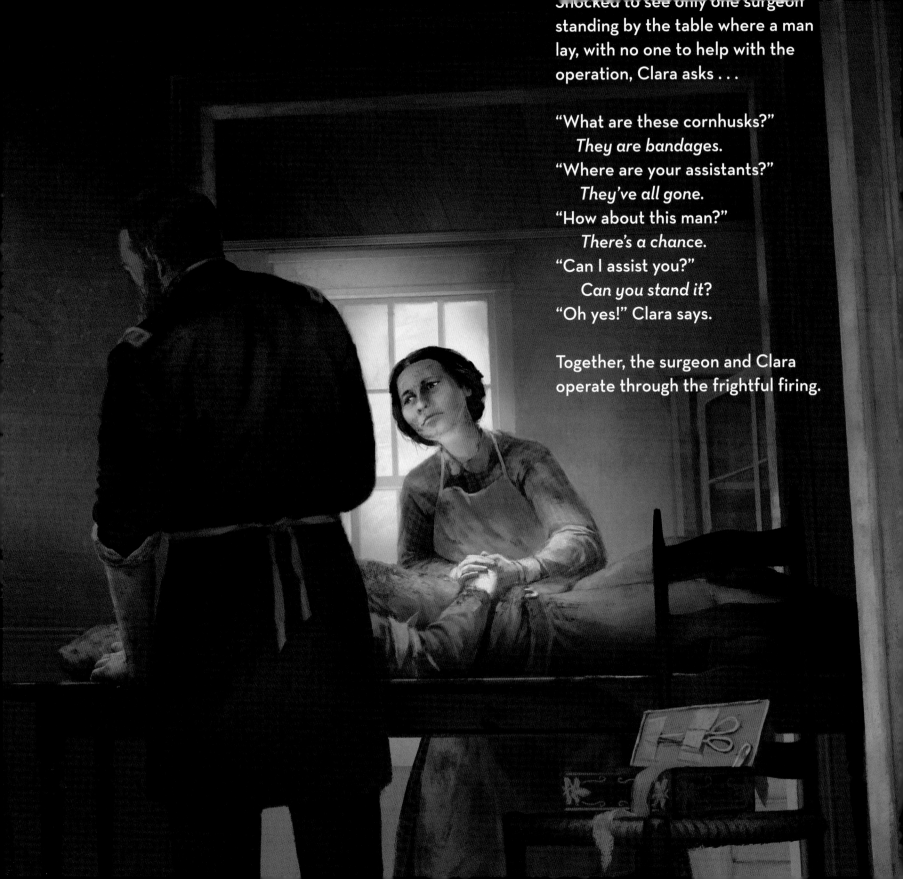

Shocked to see only one surgeon standing by the table where a man lay, with no one to help with the operation, Clara asks . . .

"What are these cornhusks?"
    They are bandages.
"Where are your assistants?"
    They've all gone.
"How about this man?"
    There's a chance.
"Can I assist you?"
    Can you stand it?
"Oh yes!" Clara says.

Together, the surgeon and Clara operate through the frightful firing.

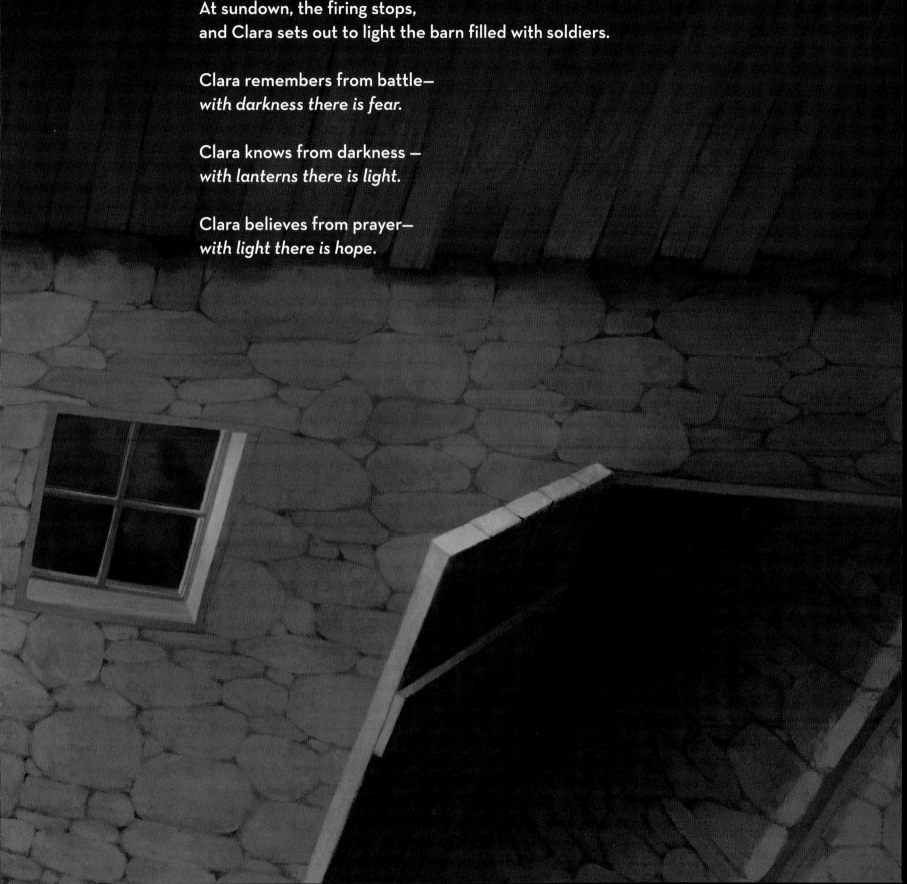

At sundown, the firing stops,
and Clara sets out to light the barn filled with soldiers.

Clara remembers from battle—
with darkness there is fear.

Clara knows from darkness —
with lanterns there is light.

Clara believes from prayer—
with light there is hope.

When I came back from the barn
I went into the house where I saw a solitary light burning.
The surgeon was sitting in one of those dark, dank rooms
with two inches of candle by him, and his head on his hand,
the picture of despair.

Clara's hand rests on the surgeon's shoulder—
You are tired, doctor.

Yes, I am tired—
tired of such carelessness,
such heartlessness,
such folly.
Tired of being left with no help,
with no light—

*"Come, doctor," said I gently
(for from my heart I pitied him),
"I want to show you something."*

I took him to the door,
and told him to look towards the barn;
it was like a garden illumination with chinese lanterns.
"What are they?" said he in amazement.
"Lanterns," said I.
"Lanterns! Where did they come from?"

"I brought them.
The men will be here in a few moments to light the house.
You will have plenty of light, and plenty of assistance.
Don't despair in your good work, doctor."

Clara keeps nursing through that long, bloody night,
keeps healing through that next dismal day,
serving until Union supplies finally come,
until Clara's things are all gone—
her strength is all gone.

They made up a bed for me of an old coverlet
on the floor of a wagon;
and I lay down on it,
and was jogged back to Washington, eighty miles.